Take Care of Yourself

Keeping Clean

D1329135

Siân Smith

www.raintreepublishers.co.uk
Visit our website to find out
more information about
Raintree books.

To order:
☎ Phone 0845 6044371
🖷 Fax +44 (0) 1865 312263
🖳 Email myorders@raintreepublishers.co.uk

Customers from outside the UK please telephone +44 1865 312262

Raintree is an imprint of Capstone Global Library Limited,
a company incorporated in England and Wales having its
registered office at 7 Pilgrim Street, London, EC4V 6LB –
Registered company number: 6695582

Text © Capstone Global Library Limited 2013
First published in hardback in 2013
First published in paperback in 2014
The moral rights of the proprietor have been asserted.

Edited by Dan Nunn, Rebecca Rissman,
   and John-Paul Wilkins
Designed by Victoria Allen
Picture research by Tracy Cummins
Production by Alison Parsons
Originated by Capstone Global Library Ltd
Printed and bound in China by Leo Paper Products Ltd

ISBN 978 1 406 24159 4 (hardback)
16 15 14 13 12
10 9 8 7 6 5 4 3 2 1

ISBN 978 1 406 24166 2 (paperback)
17 16 15 14 13
10 9 8 7 6 5 4 3 2 1

British Library Cataloguing in Publication Data
Smith, Siân.
Keeping clean. – (Take care of yourself)
613.4-dc22
A full catalogue record of this book is available from the
British Library.

Acknowledgements
We would like to thank the following for permission to
reproduce photographs: Capstone Publishers pp. 8, 21 (Karon
Dubke); Corbis pp. 7 (© Image Source), 13 (© Rubberball);
Getty Images pp. 10 (Jae Rew), 11 (Nick White), 12 (Fuse),
20 (Kohei Hara); istockphoto pp. 15 (© David Hernandez),
16 (© jianying yin), 17 (© Eric Michaud); Shutterstock pp. 4
(© Gorilla), 5, 9 (© Monkey Business Images), 6
(© 3445128471), 14 (© Catalin Petolea), 18 (© kondrytskyi),
19 (© Boris Sosnovyy), 22a (©Tina Rencelj), 22b (© Niki
Crucillo), 22c (© terekhov igor), 22d (© Nitr), 23a
(© Loskutnikov), 23b (© Grandpa).

Front cover photograph of a young girl in a bathroom
wrapped in towels reproduced with permission of Getty
Images (LM Productions). Rear cover photograph of child's
hands covered in soap reproduced with permission of
Shutterstock (© 3445128471).

Every effort has been made to contact copyright holders of
material reproduced in this book. Any omissions will be rectified
in subsequent printings if notice is given to the publisher.

We would like to thank Nancy Harris and Dee Reid for their
assistance in the preparation of this book.

Contents

Keeping clean

Everyone needs to keep clean.

Keeping clean helps you to stay healthy.

Washing your hands

Wash your hands with soap
and water.

Wash your hands all over.
Wash between your fingers, too.

You need to wash your hands
after you go to the toilet.

You need to wash your hands
before you eat.

Changing your clothes

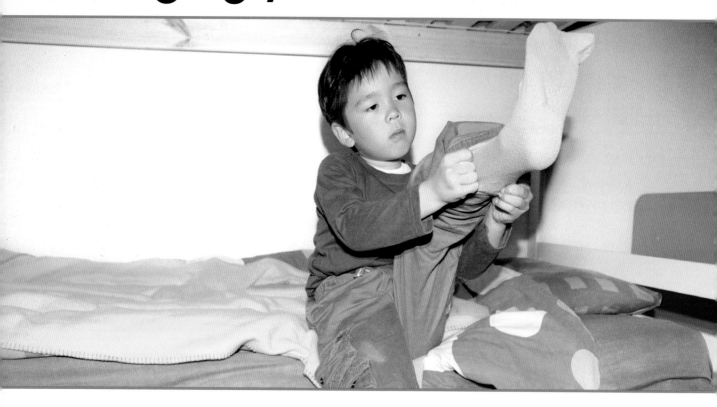

Put on clean underwear
and socks every day.

Change your other clothes often.

Don't wear clothes if you know
they are dirty.

Put them in the washing
basket instead.

Keeping your body clean

Wipe your nose with a tissue.

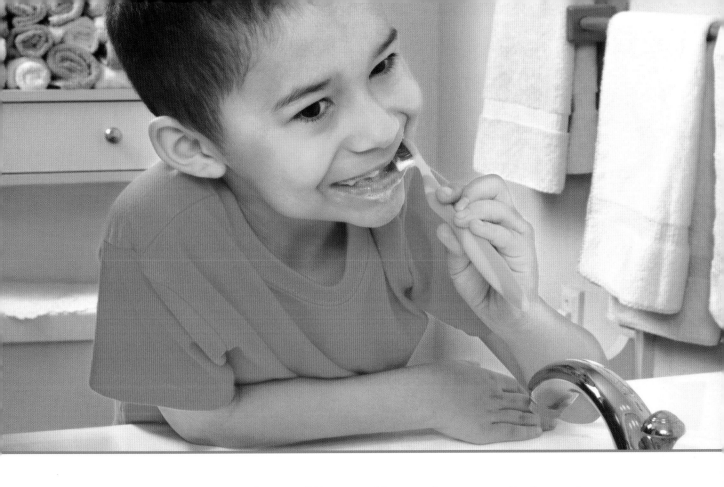

Clean your teeth after breakfast.
Clean your teeth before you sleep.

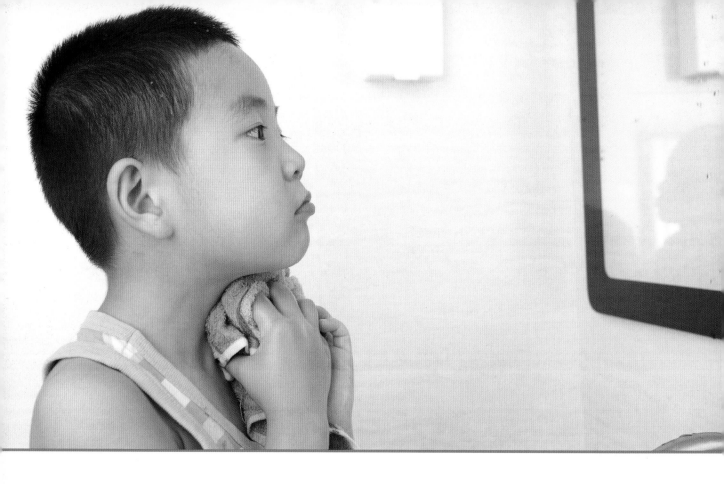

Wash your face when it gets dirty.
Wash your face before you sleep.

Have a bath or a shower every day if you can.

flannel

Clean your body with a flannel and soap.

Clean your hair with shampoo.

Then wash the shampoo away.

Make sure you clean everywhere.

Dry your body everywhere, too.

Name game

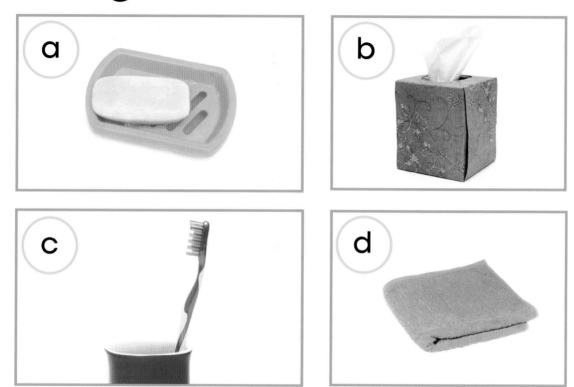

a

b

c

d

Can you name these things?

They help you to keep clean.

Answers on page 24

Picture glossary

shampoo special soap you use to wash your hair

underwear clothes you wear next to your skin under your other clothes

Index

Answers to question on page 22
a = soap   b = tissue
c = toothbrush   d = flannel

Notes for parents and teachers

Before reading

Brainstorm things we do to keep our bodies healthy. Encourage the children to think about the importance of exercise, sleep and rest, eating and drinking well, and of keeping our bodies clean and safe.

After reading

- Draw or place a picture of a person on the board and draw lines to their hair, nose, teeth, hands, and feet. Ask the children what we do to keep each of these body parts clean. Record this by writing or drawing a picture to go with each label. What do we do to keep our whole body clean?

- Children can take turns in miming something they do to keep their body clean for the others to guess. For each action ask the children if they can think of a tip to go with it, for example using a clean tissue to wipe your nose, using a nailbrush when washing your hands if you have dirt under your nails, and so on.